Bulletin Board
Activity Centers

Judy Dorsett

®
Standard Publishing
Cincinnati, Ohio   14-03284

Library of Congress Cataloging-in-Publication Data

Dorsett, Judy.
    Bulletin board activity centers / by Judy Dorsett.
      p. cm.
    ISBN 0-87403-587-2
    1. Bulletin boards in religious education.   I. Title.
    BV1535.25.D67   1989
    268'.635—dc20   89-4431
                                                              CIP

All Scripture quoted in this book is from the *International Children's Bible, New Century Version,* copyright © 1986 by Sweet Publishing, Fort Worth, Texas 76137. Used by permission.

Introduction

Need a treasure trove of ideas and activities for bulletin boards?

Here are twenty boards with more than two dozen alternative-use suggestions, plus all the patterns necessary to produce them.

With this book you can:
* Attract attention to important announcement centers

* Create seasonal boards that also have a spiritual application

* Encourage appreciation for and memorization of God's Word

* Touch class members' lives, making them feel special and honored

* Express and develop caring concern with a prayer-needs board

* Teach about God

* Actively involve children in the creation of bulletin boards with hands-on art and accompanying activities

* Improve student behavior and cooperation

* Honor parents

* Learn about missionaries

* Increase class offerings

* Promote reading of Christian material

* Adapt and use many of the forms and ideas to fit your own classroom

* Photocopy whatever you wish—as long as it's for use in your classroom and/or for related activities

LISTS ... LISTS ... LISTS

General Education

Learning to Obey God
A Great Review

Prayer

Prayer Has Wings
Summertime Prayer Needs

Bible Memorization

The Best Book
"Berry" Good Memorization
Winter WonderVERSES
A Child's Garden of Verses

Christian Reading/Library

Book Nook
Summertime Reading
Berry Good Books

Religious Seasonal

Easter—Jesus Lives!
Christmas—Jesus, Light of the World

Behavior Recognition

"Berry" Good Deeds
"Berry" Good Behavior
Winter WonderKIDS
Winter WonderDEEDS

Secular Seasonal—spiritual application

Jesus in My Heart! (Valentine's Day)
For Mom or May
For Dad
Summertime
Jesus, Rose of Sharon
THANKSgiving
Winter WonderKIDS

Offering

A Piggy Bank for Jesus
A Money Tree for Jesus

Announcements

"Berry" Good News
"Berry" Good Notes
Summertime Activities
Summertime Announcements
Summertime in Review
Winter Wonderful Events

Birthday

"Berry" Good Birthday
Winter Wonderful Birthdays

Multi-use materials

Floral Note Form, page 29
Seat Reserved Ticket, page 48
Calendar Blank, page 62
Greeting Card Blank, page 63
Puzzle Blank, page 64

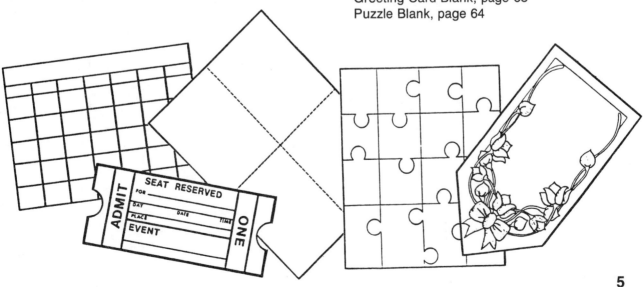

 # MAKING BORDERS

Borders!   Whether finishing the edges, following through on a board theme, adding a 3-D effect, or highlighting board colors, borders improve a bulletin board's overall effect.

Border Variety!   It's endless—limited only by our imaginations.

Here are a few ideas:

* Paper shapes—scallops, icicles, fringes, bears, feet, hands, lace, music notes, etc.

* Student artwork—seasonal items such as snowflakes, leaves, hearts, Easter lilies; any other item children create that would make a nice border—handprints, other flowers, and so on

* Crepe paper streamers—¾" wide, twisted, and stapled to board

* Rope or braid

* Artificial silk flowers and leaves

* Pre-made borders—purchased from educational stores

New in this book; Folded paper borders!
Remember cutting out rows of paper dolls?
These borders are just as easy and save lots of preparation time.
You'll find this type of border in "Jesus in my Heart," "Prayer Has Wings!" "For Mom or May," "A Child's Garden of Verses," and "Winter WonderKIDS."

Here's how to make these borders:

* Cut a long strip of paper. Make it as tall as the height of the pattern.

* Fold the paper, accordion fashion. Make folds the width of the pattern you are using.

* Make a master pattern from tagboard or some other heavy paper. Lay it on the top fold of the paper strip, making sure that your pattern extends to both folds. Trace around it.

* Cut away the excess paper, being careful not to cut the fold sections that join the pattern parts. Unfold and pin to board. Enjoy!

USING PATTERNS

Scattered throughout this book you will find many patterns. Here is one way these can be copied:

Place a sheet of carbon paper (carbon side down) over a piece of tagboard (heavy manilla-folder type paper, sold in art and educational supply stores). Slip these in under the page containing the pattern(s) to be copied.

Trace over the pattern with heavy strokes. Use a blunt-ended object such as a crochet hook to avoid marking the pattern or ripping the page.

Remove carbon paper and tagboard, and cut out the patterns that now appear on the tagboard. They are ready for students or teacher to trace around.

Pages fifty-eight through sixty-one, shown on this page, are designed for overhead projector use. Transparencies may be prepared in either of two ways:

✻ Trace the patterns onto a clear transparency sheet with any ink pen designed for writing on plastic. (A washable pen will allow you to make corrections.)

✻ Tear the pages out. Have an overhead transparency made of each one of them. Office supply stores will do this if you do not have access to a copier that makes transparencies.

When you have the transparencies, place the design you wish to enlarge on an overhead projector. Move the projector forward or backward to adjust pattern to correct size. Project the board parts and letters onto colored paper on the actual board you are designing. Just remember to put newsprint underneath the paper on which you are tracing. Marker ink will sometimes seep through onto the bulletin board base or wall being used. After you have traced these parts, leave the transparency and overhead projector exactly where they are. When you have cut out and assembled board parts and letters, you may reuse the projected image of the board design to assure correct placement of pattern pieces.

Letter patterns—either copied from this book, or from some you have—may also be enlarged with an overhead projector. Project the letters onto the colored board or paper you have chosen, trace around their shadow shapes, cut them out, and attach them to the board.

LEARNING TO OBEY GOD

JONAH 1-3

Suggestions:

Background—blue
Waves—blue and white
Fish—gray
Letters—black, dark blue, or white
Fish pattern for enlarging on page fifty-eight

Word search puzzle to accompany lesson and bulletin board, page nine.

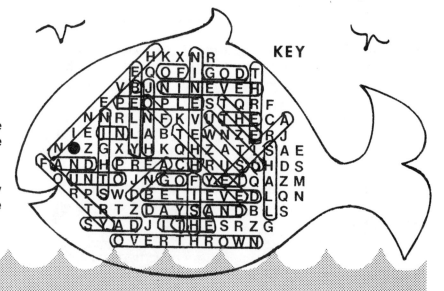

KEY

A Fish Tale

Directions: Use a different color pencil for each verse. Circle each word from the verses that you find in this word search puzzle.

1. "Yet forty days and Nineveh shall be over-thrown."
   —Jonah 3:4

2. "Arise, go unto Nineveh . . . and preach unto it. . . ."
   —Jonah 3:2

3. "Jonah was in the belly of the fish three days and three nights."
   —Jonah 1:17

4. "The people of Nineveh believed God."
   —Jonah 3:5

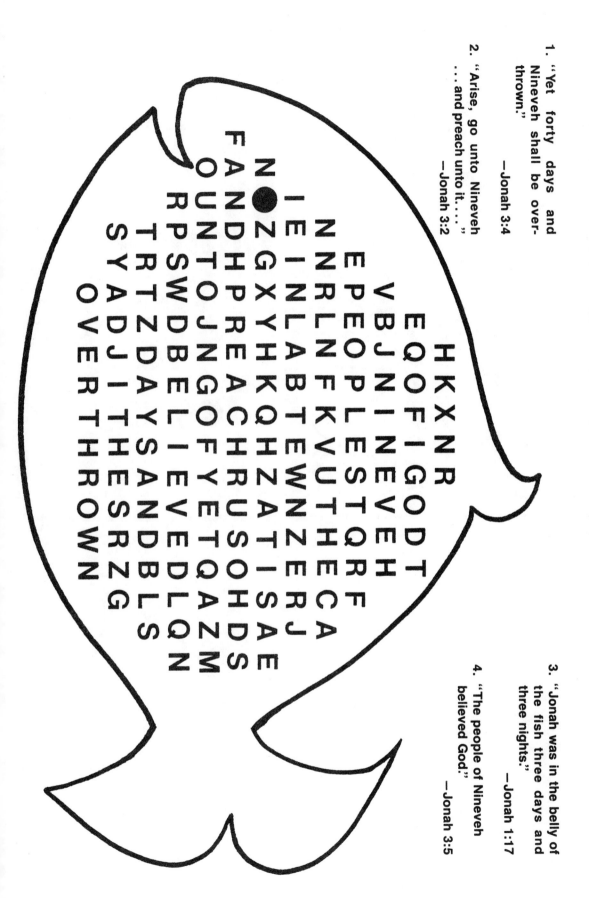

A Money Tree for Jesus

Suggestions:

Background—blue

Branches—real branches slant pinned to board *or* paper branches stapled to board

Leaves—two shades of green paper for spring or summer, with dollar signs printed on them
—red, orange, yellow, or brown leaves for autumn
—tape or hot glue leaves to branches; each leaf represents one dollar given.

Letters—brown paper, patterns here and on page sixty-one

Small leaves for letters—same colors as big leaves, no dollar signs printed on them

Suggested use—offering emphasis. Students try to reach an offering goal, or raise funds for a special occasion, or for a mission project.

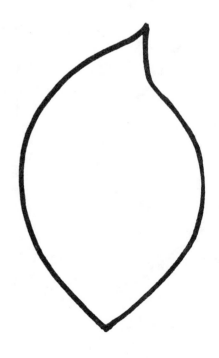

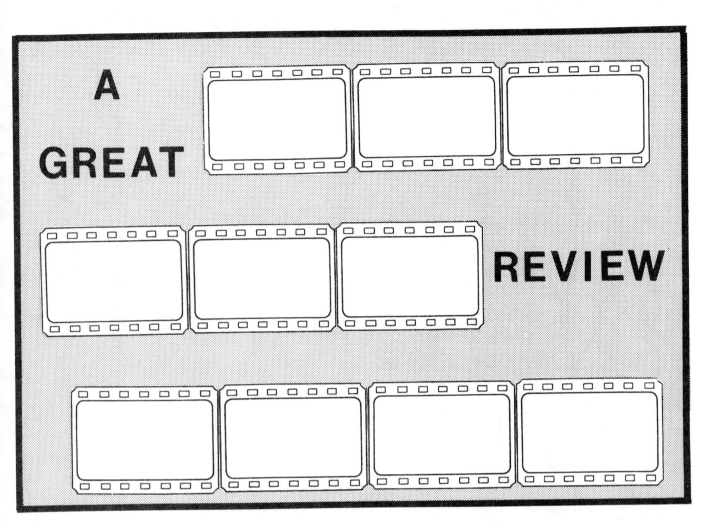

A GREAT REVIEW

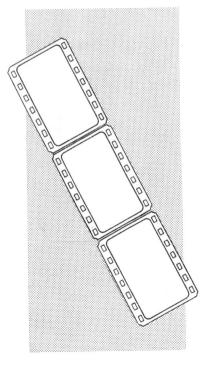

Suggestions:

Background—any color
Letters—complimentary color to background
Slide forms—white, pattern on page twelve

With the class, plan eight to ten pictures that show the sequence of events in a story. Each child or small group draws one picture in a slide form. Place the pictures on the board in the correct order.

Story ideas: The birth of Jesus, His death and resurrection, life of any Bible character, missionary journeys of Paul, calling of Samuel, etc.

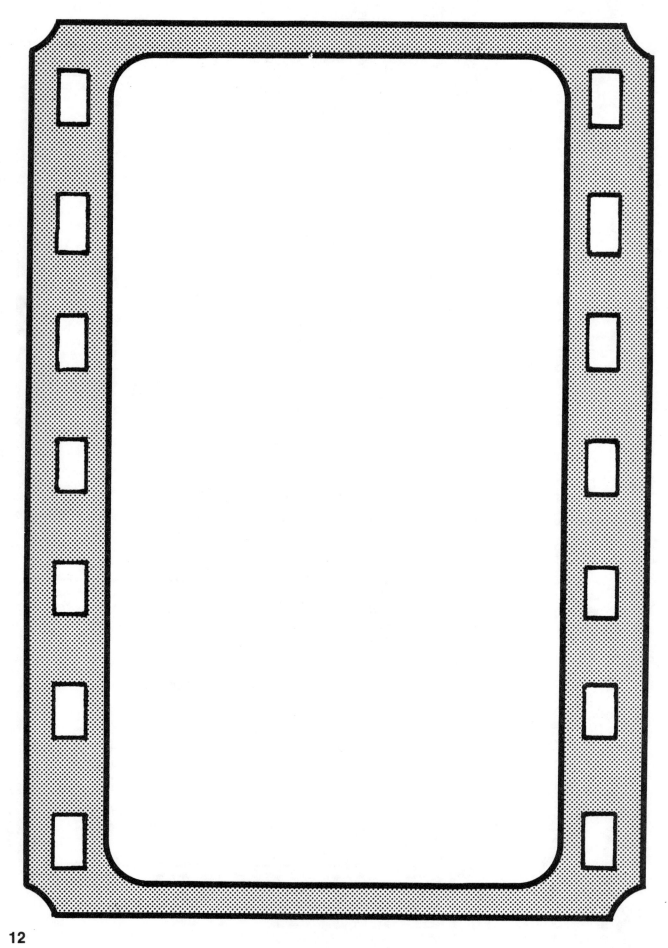

Suggestions:

Background—pink

Border—red paper strips, prepared as directed on page fourteen

Letters—black, red

Hearts—red construction paper, white photocopies of page fifteen, tagboard for the double-heart pattern on page fourteen, and a felt-tip pen for writing names on the hearts.

Directions: Make hearts as instructed on pages fourteen and fifteen. Do this a week or two before Valentine's Day to extend board time. Pin hearts to board. Students may take the hearts home either on Valentine's Day or after the following class session.

Jesus in My Heart

Cut out.

He
loves
you

Fold on dotted lines.

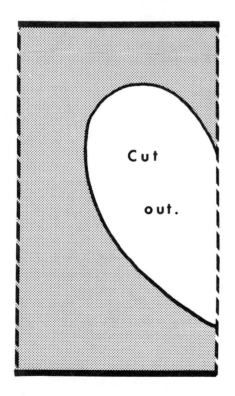

Cut out.

Instructions for making border:

Cut long strips of red paper 4½″ wide, to fit around your bulletin board. Fold each strip accordion fashion, at 3⅝ inch intervals—as pattern shows.

Make a tagboard heart pattern. Place it in the center of the 4½ inch square and trace around it. Cut hearts out, and unfold the strips. If the folded paper is too thick to cut, simply do a section at a time, and tape the sections back together (place tape on underneath side) before placing on the board.

(To make your hearts "topside up" all the way around the board, place the top and bottom of the heart facing the *folds* for your side strips, and facing the *edges* for your top and bottom strips.)

Save the cut out heart shapes for use on this board, or other Valentine's Day uses.

Jesus in My Heart!

Trace this shape onto several pieces of tagboard. Cut out, remembering to remove the diamond shape between the two hearts. Students trace around this shape on red construction paper, cut out the hearts, and fold them in half. Students write their names on the front heart. Glue a "Jesus in my Heart!" shape (pattern on page sixteen) onto the inside heart. (Use rubber cement or glue stick so the paper won't pucker.)

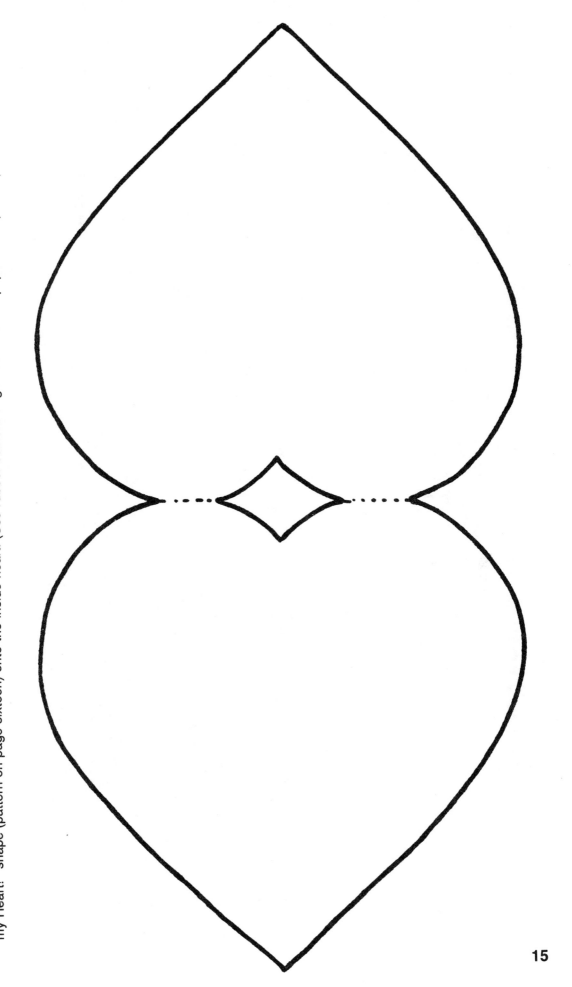

15

Jesus in My Heart!

Make enough photocopies of this page to give each student one "Jesus in My Heart!" form to cut out and paste inside the red, folded construction paper heart made from the pattern on page fifteen.

Suggestions:

Background—brown

Bird border—light or bright blue

Prayer request forms—copies on page twenty

Letters—yellow, black, or blue

Prayer Calendars—Make one copy of page nineteen for each student. Fill in the month name and numbers for younger students. Older class members can fill in that information themselves. Display a sample of the calendar with correct number placement.

PRAYER

HAS

WINGS!

Prayer Calendar

Send calendar home with class members so they can keep a daily record of their prayer time.

Tell students to put the calendar in a spot they see each day so they will remember to mark it.

Teacher may wish to give a small reward to each student who returns the calendar at the month's end.

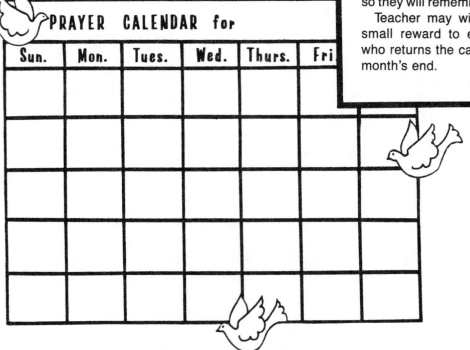

PRAYER CALENDAR for

Sun.	Mon.	Tues.	Wed.	Thurs.	Fri

PRAYER CALENDAR for

Sun.	Mon.	Tues.	Wed.	Thurs.	Fri.	Sat.

Prayer request

_____
_____
_____
_____
from_____

Prayer request

_____
_____
_____
_____
from_____

Prayer request

_____
_____
_____
_____
from_____

Jesus Lives!

Suggestions:
Background—blue, yellow, or light green
Letters—black or brown

Lilies—white paper, yellow pipe cleaners
Leaves—dark green, cut to look like lily leaves

Lily instructions: Children place their hand on white paper with all the digits pointing in the same direction. (If the digits are too spread out, petals of the lily will crisscross.) Trace around the hand, making fingers as wide as possible, with pointed tips. Cut out. Curl finger and thumb parts outward. Roll into a funnel-like shape. Curl top ends of yellow pipe cleaners into small circle shapes to make stamens. Insert the straight end of two or three of these pipe cleaners into base of lily-funnel shape. Staple lily by its base to the board. Add leaves.

Students color the stained-glass window pictures (page twenty-two) for the board. Extra copies may be cut out and taped to a window. Students may also want to tape their pictures to windows when they take them home.

NAME

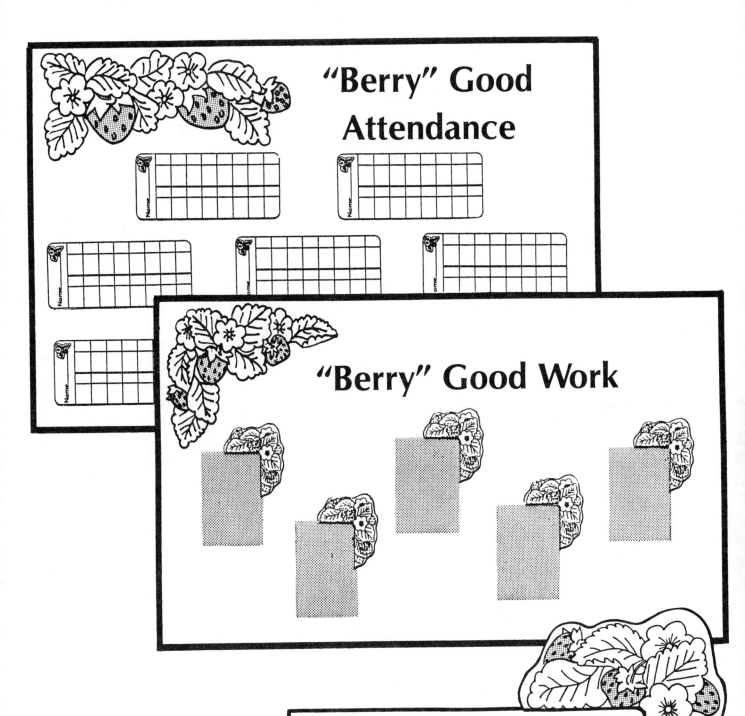

"Berry" Good Attendance

"Berry" Good Work

Related Titles:

"Berry" Good Books

"Berry" Good Deeds

"Berry" Good Art

"Berry" Good Ideas

"Berry" Good Behavior

"Berry" Good Memorization

"Berry" Good News

"Berry" Good Notes

"Berry" Good Birthdays

Suggestions:

Background—blue or light green

Leaves—dark green, lighter green for hull

Berries—red, with black marker

Flowers—white, with yellow marker

Letters—dark green or black

Corner decorations—pattern on page twenty-four

Children may color their corner piece and put their names on the back. Attach papers, attendance or memory-work forms, books, idea sheets, or art work to corner decorations and place on board.

"Berry" Good

Strawberry Patterns
Hull, berry, leaves, and flower

Corner Decoration
Fasten student's paper here.

Uses for chart:

"Berry" Good Attendance

Trim one row of squares off the right side of the chart so it has seven rows left. Write the date for each class meeting during the quarter in the small slot. Use a check mark, colored sticker, or star in the large slot for each time student attends.

"Berry" Good Memorization

Chart has enough slots for thirteen verses and three extra-credit verses. Write the verse reference in the small slot. Fill larger slot in with a check, colored sticker, or star when student learns each verse.

"Berry" Good Deeds

Use to record the positive things students do for others such as: helping with memory verses, being friendly to a visitor, helping the teacher, helping set up the classroom, finishing work, helping to clean up, and so on. Date the occasion in the small slot and place the "reward sticker" in the large slot.

"Berry" Good Behavior

Use in a fashion similar to "Berry" Good Deeds, except reward improved behaviors. Each student may have their own individual goals you have mutually agreed on such as: being cheerful, cooperative, kind to others, neat, quiet during story, or taking part in discussion. Whenever the desired behavior is practiced, note the occasion on the student's chart.

Corner decorations are attached to right side of each student's chart and placed on the board.

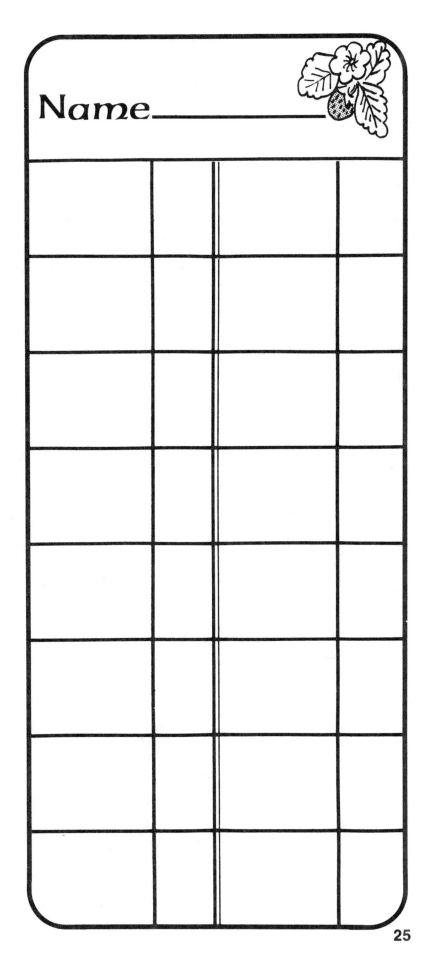

Name_____

"Berry" Good Birthday!

Directions: Teacher fills in birthday information and pins this card to the bulletin board. On the birthday celebration day, child is given his/her card, which he/she can color, cut out, and put together again.

Have a "Berry" Good Birthday!

to _____

from _____

26

For Mom or May

Background—blue

Flowers—yellow, pink, and/or white, pattern on page twenty-eight

Leaves—green, pattern on page twenty-eight.

Note forms—copies of page twenty-nine

Bow border—yellow, pink, pattern on page twenty-eight

Large bow—same color as border, pattern (to be enlarged) on page fifty-eight.

Letters—one of the flower colors, pattern on page sixty-one

Special Instructions:

Teacher prepares board and makes copies of note forms.
Children write their message on the form, color it if they wish, and cut it out. See page thirty for sample messages, or children may compose their own. Prepare two or three weeks in advance. Then send the notes home with children on Mother's Day. Those who don't have a mother in the home may make the note for a grandmother or aunt—or choose not to make one.

Alternate use: After Mother's Day,
　　　　　　　pin up spring scene pictures.

For Mom or May

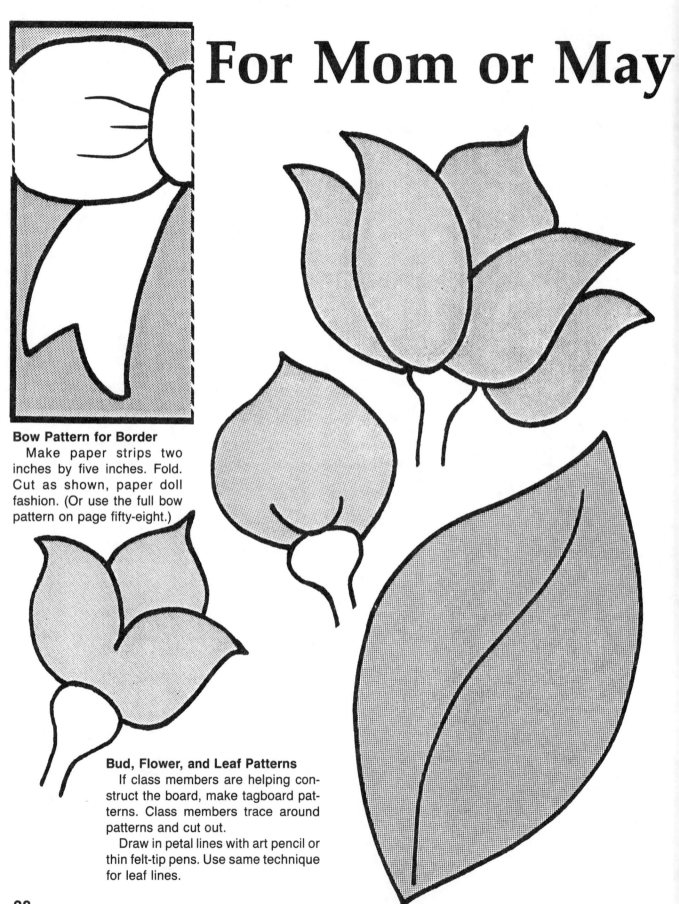

Bow Pattern for Border

Make paper strips two inches by five inches. Fold. Cut as shown, paper doll fashion. (Or use the full bow pattern on page fifty-eight.)

Bud, Flower, and Leaf Patterns

If class members are helping construct the board, make tagboard patterns. Class members trace around patterns and cut out.

Draw in petal lines with art pencil or thin felt-tip pens. Use same technique for leaf lines.

Instructions: Make as many copies of this page as are needed for class members, plus a few extra in case of student mistakes.

Students write their message to Mother on the form, color the flowers, stems, and bow—if they wish. Then, students cut out the form and teacher pins it to the board.

Some sample messages are given on the next page if children have difficulty thinking of one of their own to write.

Alternate uses:

Invitations to Mother's Day events

Invitations to May or spring events

Invitations to ladies' events

Thank you notes

This form, if copied on a machine that enlarges, can be increased to full page size for whatever use one likes.

Notes for Mom and Dad

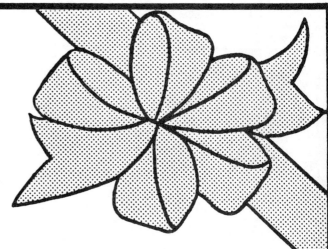

Directions: Copy these sample notes to Mom and Dad *or* write your own message on the Mother's Day or Father's Day card (pattern on page thirty-two).

Dear Father,
This special day
lets me tell you
how much I love you.
Thanks for being
a great dad!
Love,

Dear Dad,
Everyone deserves a
father as neat as you!
You take care of me,
love me, and
we have fun together.
Your grateful (son/daughter),

Dear Mother,
You are the best mom
anyone could have.
You love me,
take care of me,
and teach me about God.
Thank you!
Hugs and kisses,

Dear Mom,
You are a great mom!
Thanks for taking care of me,
loving me, and
having fun with me.
I love you, too.
Lots of love,

Suggestions:

Background—medium blue, medium green, or brown

Ribbon—red, enlarged from pattern on page fifty-eight

Letters—black

Cards—Father's Day cards made from pattern on page thirty-two,
      prepared by students

Instructions:

Children each color a copy of Father's Day card from page thirty-two. They write in their own message or use one from page thirty, or one provided by teacher. Cards are cut out and folded. Pin cards to the board until the class ends. Teacher may use this activity a week or two ahead of Father's Day for longer board use.

Some children may wish to make the card for Grandpa—or choose not to make a card if there is no father in the home.

DAD

Happy
Father's
Day

A Piggy Bank for Jesus

Offering Game or Contest

Suggestions:
    Background—white, lime, or blue
    Pig—pink
    Flower—white
    Leaves—green
    Letters—black, enlarged and cut out from patterns on page fifty-nine

Directions: Enlarge entire board to correct size from this page or patterns on page fifty-nine. Trace around pig, flower, and leaves with a pencil on appropriately colored paper. Outline with black felt-tip pen, cut out, and glue flower and leaves to pig.

    Photocopy piggy bank money from page thirty-four onto green paper. Cut out. Staple to pig as group contributes each dollar amount. Set a goal for the class to reach. Teacher may keep actual count of money given or may round up or down the amount this way: $1.49 equals one piggy bank dollar, $1.51 equals two piggy bank dollars.

Piggy Bank Money

Photocopy onto green paper.
Cut out.

Book Nook

Suggestions:

Background—blue

Sign—black for wrought iron
    tan for hanging shingle
    black for letters

Plant stand—brown paper with
    black lines drawn to resemble
    wood grain

Plant pot—any color

Plant leaves—green paper, or silk
    leaves

Patterns on page sixty are to be enlarged

Books—Use real books, appropriate to the age level of your students. Slant heavy
    pins into the bulletin board and rest the books on the pins. A pin on the top,
    slanted up into the board, will keep the books from falling. Class members
    may slide the books out from between the pins.

Change books every week or two to maintain interest.

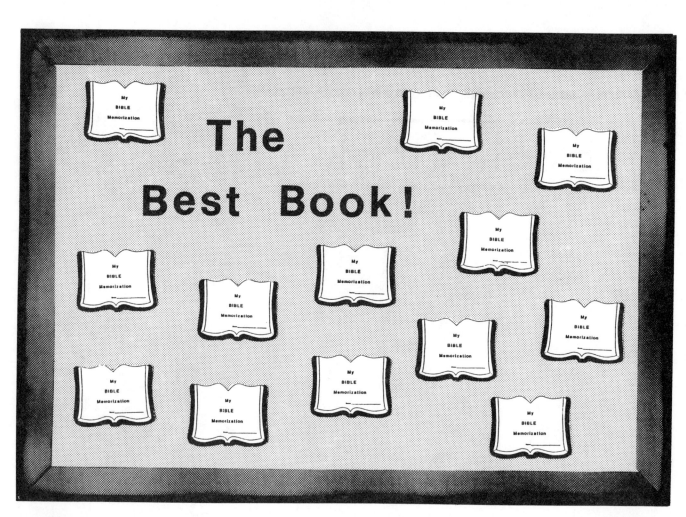

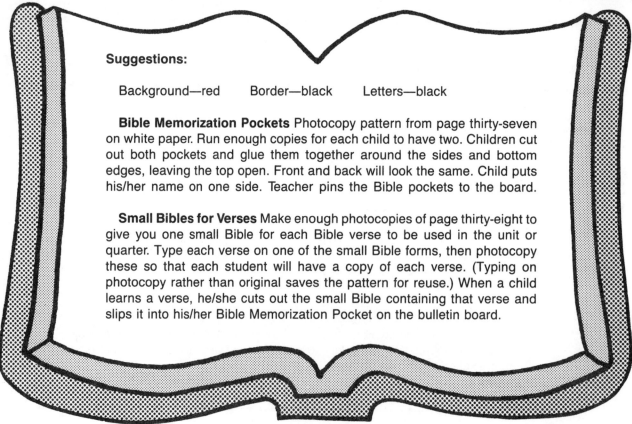

Suggestions:

Background—red   Border—black   Letters—black

Bible Memorization Pockets Photocopy pattern from page thirty-seven on white paper. Run enough copies for each child to have two. Children cut out both pockets and glue them together around the sides and bottom edges, leaving the top open. Front and back will look the same. Child puts his/her name on one side. Teacher pins the Bible pockets to the board.

Small Bibles for Verses Make enough photocopies of page thirty-eight to give you one small Bible for each Bible verse to be used in the unit or quarter. Type each verse on one of the small Bible forms, then photocopy these so that each student will have a copy of each verse. (Typing on photocopy rather than original saves the pattern for reuse.) When a child learns a verse, he/she cuts out the small Bible containing that verse and slips it into his/her Bible Memorization Pocket on the bulletin board.

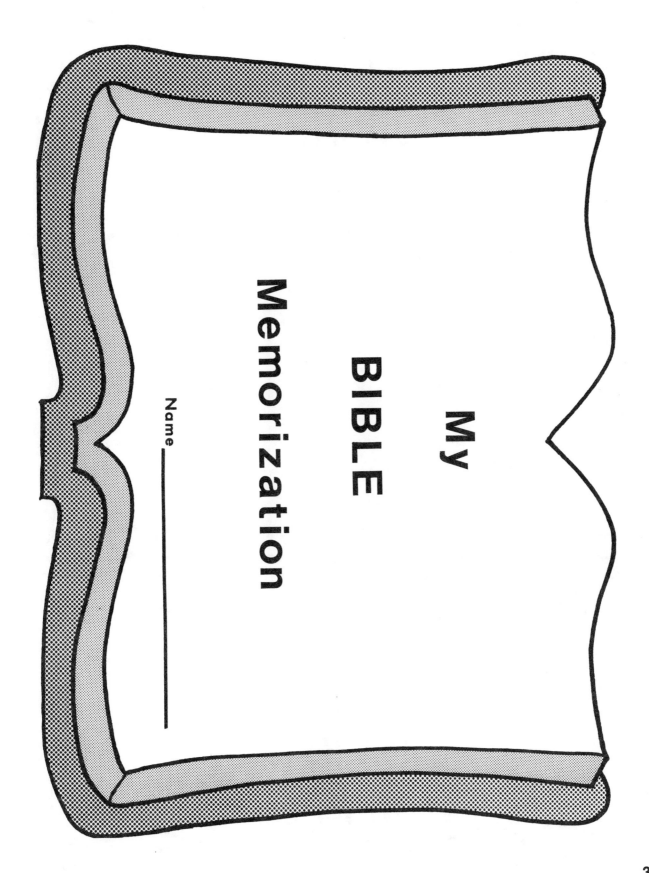

My

BIBLE

Memorization

Name

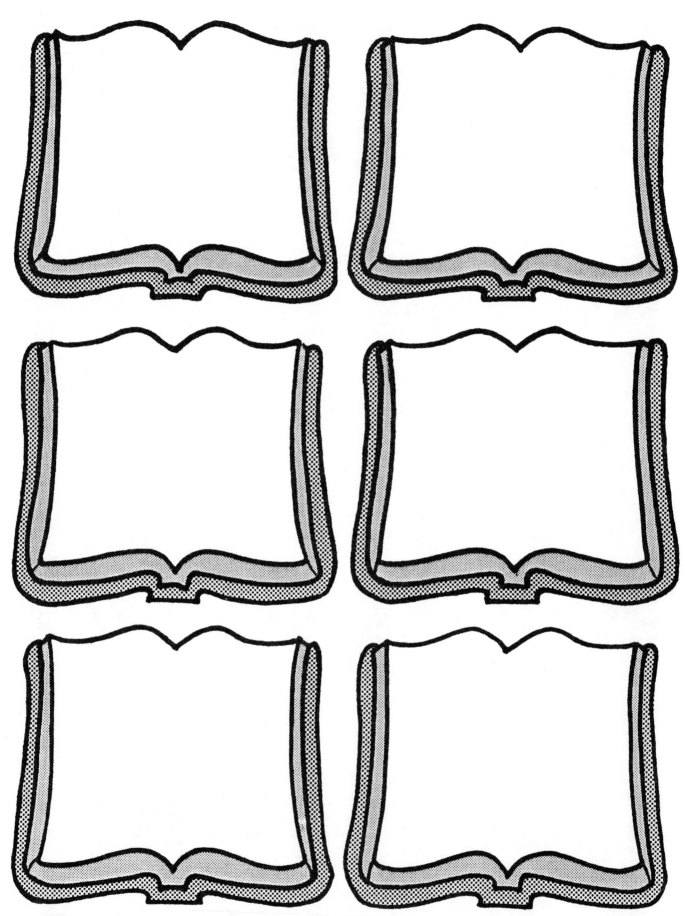

Jesus, Rose of Sharon

Suggested uses:

General purpose board for spring, summer, or fall
Church office
Adult classroom
Fellowship area
Hallway

Background—blue

Leaves—medium green

Stems and thorns—black marking pen, drawn onto background

Letters—black paper, enlarge and trace the pattern on page sixty, cut out

Roses—pink for spring, red for summer, yellow or orange for fall—pattern on page sixty

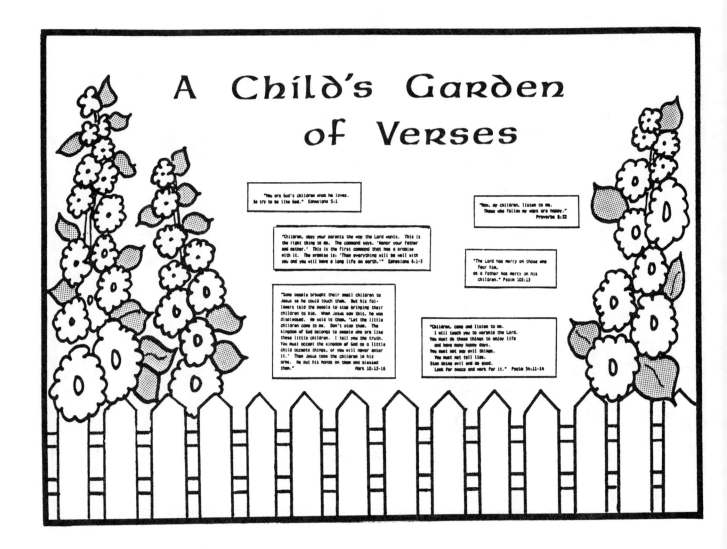

A Display of Bible verses relating to children and/or growing in God

Background—blue

Letters—black or dark green, patterns on page sixty-one

Flowers—shades of pink to rose

Leaves—green, patterns on page forty-two

Fence—white, patterns on page forty-three. Fold and cut out paper-doll fashion. Two different size patterns are provided.

Verse cards—3-inch × 5-inch, or 4-inch × 6-inch cards with verses typed or printed on them.

Suggestions:
✳ To involve children in board construction, make tagboard patterns of flower and leaf shapes. Children trace around and cut out. Teacher assembles.
✳ Change verse cards every two or three weeks to keep board interesting.
✳ Some verses are provided on page forty-one. A quarter's memory verses may be used instead.

Alternate use suggestion: Omit the word "Child's" to make the board an all-purpose one, using Bible verses for any theme. This makes it practical for church offices, hallways, fellowship rooms, or general areas.

A Child's Garden of Verses

"You are God's children whom he loves. So try to be like God."

—Ephesians 5:1

"The Lord has mercy on those who fear him,
as a father has mercy on his children."

Psalm 103:13

"Some people brought their small children to Jesus so he could touch them. But his followers told the people to stop bringing their children to him. When Jesus saw this, he was displeased. He said to them, 'Let the little children come to me. Don't stop them. The kingdom of God belongs to people who are like these little children. I tell you the truth. You must accept the kingdom of God as a little child accepts things, or you will never enter it.' Then Jesus took the children in his arms. He put his hands on them and blessed them." Mark 10:13-16

"Children, obey your parents the way the Lord wants. This is the right thing to do. The command says, 'Honor your father and mother.' This is the first command that has a promise with it. The promise is: 'Then everything will be well with you, and you will have a long life on the earth.'"

Ephesians 6:1-3

"Children, come and listen to me.
  I will teach you to worship the Lord.
You must do these things to enjoy life
  and have many happy days.
You must not say evil things.
  You must not tell lies.
Stop doing evil and do good.
  Look for peace and work for it."

Psalm 34:11-14

"Children are a gift from the Lord.
Babies are a reward."

Psalm 127:3

"Now, my children, listen to me.
  Those who follow my ways are happy.

Proverbs 8:32

Patterns for "A Child's Garden of Verses"

Hollyhock leaf pattern

Hollyhock flower patterns

Fence Border

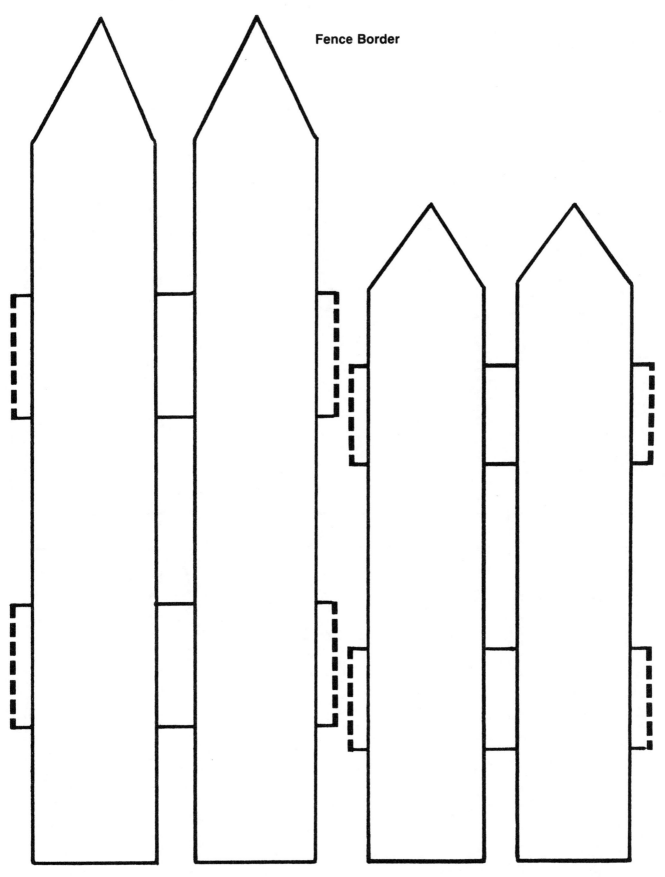

For use on boards thirty-six inches tall.
Fold paper into 9-inch by 3-inch sections.

For use on boards twenty-four inches tall.
Fold paper into 7-inch by 3¼-inch sections.

Summertime

Suggestions:

Sun border—orange

Sun face—yellow

Nose and cheeks—orange

Eyes—white with black felt-tip pen

Eyebrows—black felt-tip pen

Smile—black felt-tip pen

Letters—black paper

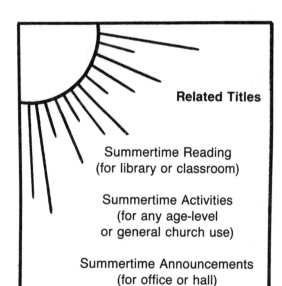

Enlarge the sun pattern from page fifty-eight. Trace with pencil. Outline sun with black felt-tip pen. Cut out. Glue sun parts together with rubber cement or glue stick.

Letter patterns for "Summertime" are on page sixty-one, or you may choose to use your own patterns so that the entire title is in the same type style.

Related Titles

Summertime Reading
(for library or classroom)

Summertime Activities
(for any age-level
or general church use)

Summertime Announcements
(for office or hall)

Summertime in Review
(photograph display)

Summertime Prayer Needs

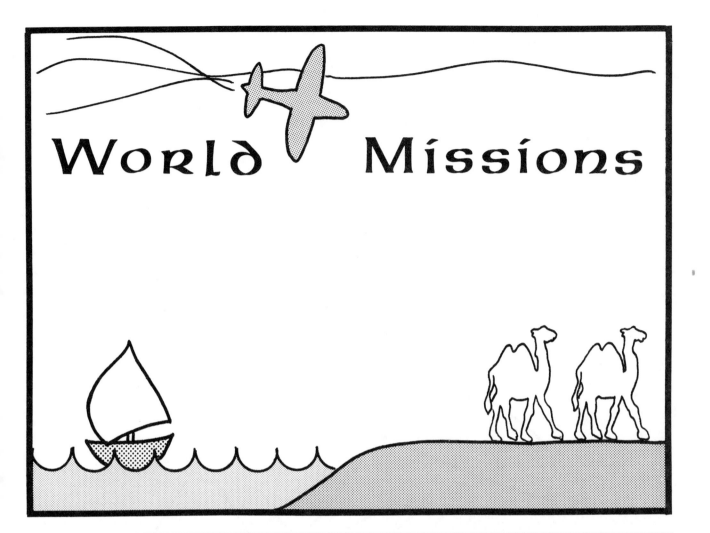

World Missions

Use for pictures of missionaries, letters from missionaries, or missionary lessons.

Background—blue

Water—darker blue

Sand—tan

Airplane—grey

Boat—brown for boat, white for sail

Camels—brown or gold

Letters—black

Flight lines—felt-tip pen drawn on background.

Use patterns on next page for small boards or enlarge patterns from pages fifty-nine and sixty-one for larger boards.

If children are writing to missionaries, post their letters on the board for two or three weeks before mailing them.

This board can be used in classrooms, work areas for missionary projects, church offices, hallways, or wherever missionary news is posted.

Patterns for "World Missions" Board

If the mission reports, lesson pictures, or letters to missionaries feature a part of the world where only one of these types of travel is appropriate, just use the one pattern to adapt the board.

Fly the plane across the sky, or use only the boat and water, or the camel and sand. An example of how to use the camel and sand is in the instruction section on page forty-five.

46

World Missions

To add interest in the lesson, set the chairs in the shape of some mode of travel mentioned or implied in the missionary lesson, such as an airplane, camel, or ship.

The block diagrams on this page represent seating arrangements for class member's chairs. Smaller arrangements are possible for the airplane and ship. With some adaptations to the camel, one can create a mule or a horse.

If the missionary encounters stormy weather, younger students enjoy rocking back and forth and making wind and storm sounds.

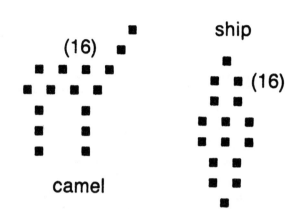

ship

camel

airplane

Admission Ticket

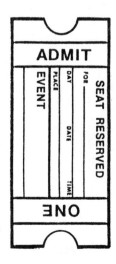

＊Photocopy the tickets (page forty-eight) onto colored paper, if possible. Cut the tickets apart. Fill in the student's name, date, and place of missionary lesson. On the "Event" line, write something like, "Trip to Rome," "Journey to Indonesia," or "Travel to India."

＊Mail tickets to students, instructing them to bring them on Sunday. Have extra on hand in case students forget to bring them to class.

＊Alternate method: hand tickets out at door when class members arrive.

＊These tickets may be used for other church-related events.

SEAT RESERVED

ADMIT

FOR _____

DAY   DATE   TIME

PLACE

EVENT

ONE

SEAT RESERVED

ADMIT

FOR _____

DAY   DATE   TIME

PLACE

EVENT

ONE

SEAT RESERVED

ADMIT

FOR _____

DAY   DATE   TIME

PLACE

EVENT

ONE

THANKSgiving

'THANKS' giving
to_____
from_____

"O Lord my God, I will give thanks unto thee for ever."
Psalm 30:12

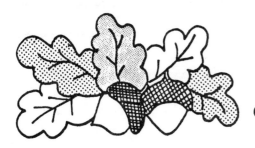

THANKSgiving

Children write thank-you letters to God for His love and goodness during this year.

Background—gold

Border—oak leaves—orange, yellow, rust, brown, green acorns—tan for bottom, darker brown for top. Draw lines across top as shown. Patterns on page fifty-one. Students may trace and cut out.

Letters—brown or black, patterns on page sixty-one.

THANKSgiving form—patterns on page fifty. Children may color these.

THANKSgiving

to _____

_____

_____

from _____

THANKSgiving

to _____

_____

_____

from _____

THANKSgiving

to _____

_____

_____

from _____

Patterns for THANKSgiving Board

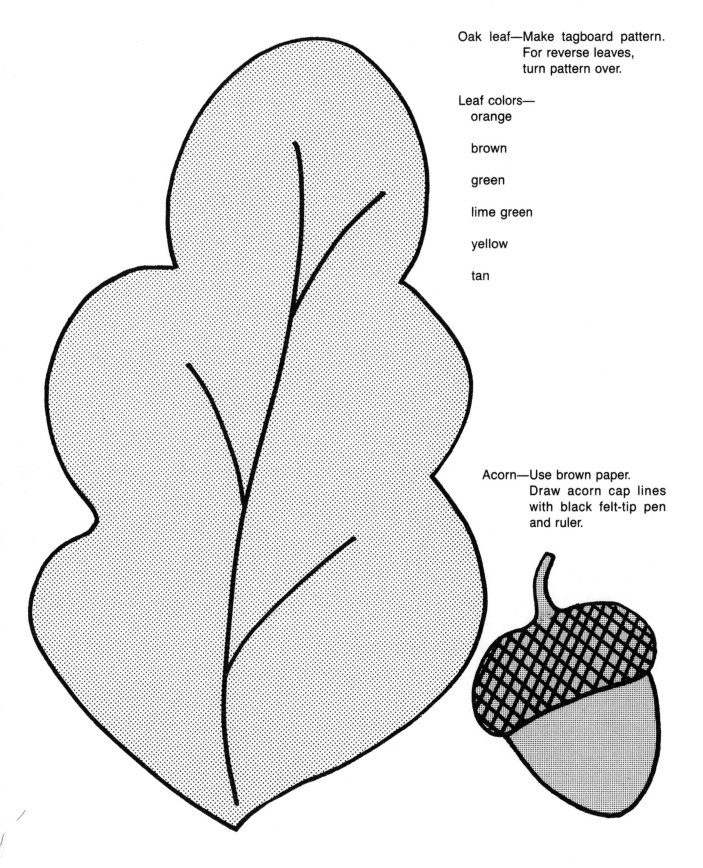

Oak leaf—Make tagboard pattern.
For reverse leaves,
turn pattern over.

Leaf colors—
   orange

   brown

   green

   lime green

   yellow

   tan

Acorn—Use brown paper.
   Draw acorn cap lines
   with black felt-tip pen
   and ruler.

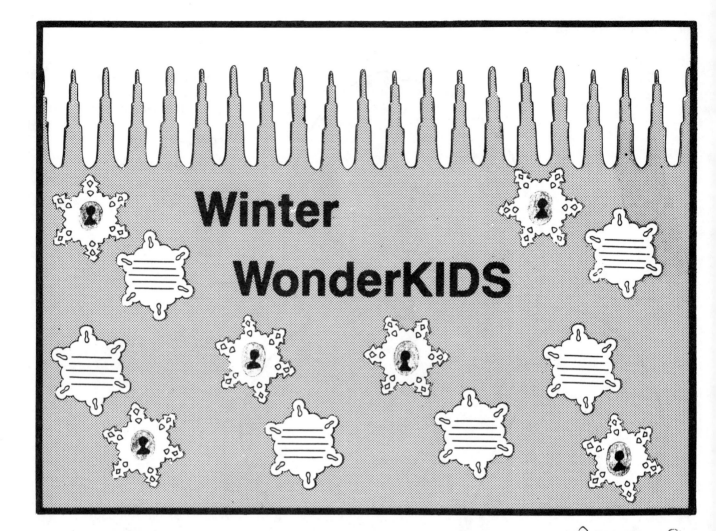

Winter WonderKIDS

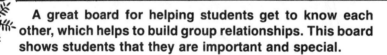

A great board for helping students get to know each other, which helps to build group relationships. This board shows students that they are important and special.

Background—dark blue

Icicle border—white folded paper, pattern on page fifty-three

Letters—red paper, pattern on page sixty-one

Snowflakes—photocopy page fifty-four, one page for each class member. Cut out snowflakes, or allow older students to cut out their own flakes. Attach pictures to the blank snowflakes, and write student info on the lined snowflakes.

Pictures—Use small school photos or photos you take. Stand two children a foot or so from each other against a blank wall. When pictures are developed, you can cut them in half and shape them as desired to fit within the flake. This is less expensive than taking individual pictures of each student.

Information—On first line write the student's name. Use other lines for such things as: favorite Bible story, hobbies, school attended, favorite song or book, etc.

Winter WonderKIDS

Enjoy many variations of this winter bulletin board:

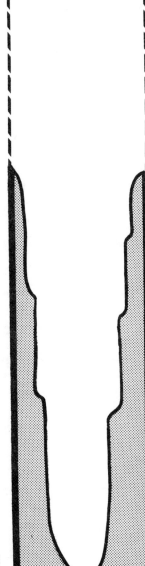

Icicle pattern for large
bulletin boards

Icicle pattern for small
bulletin boards

✳**Winter Wonderful Birthdays**

Use pictures of class members whose birthdays fall within the month—or within the quarter—on the blank snowflakes. On the lined snowflake, write the student's name and birthday information. Change month by month, or quarter by quarter.

✳**Winter WonderDEEDS**

Put pictures of people to be honored on blank snowflakes. Write the name of the good deed or achievement forwhich they are being honored on lined flake.

✳**Winter Wonderful Events**

Type event information on the blank snowflake or print it on the lined flake. Great for hallways, office, or general area boards.

✳**Winter WonderVERSES**

Print verses on lined flakes or type on blank flake forms. Use for a unit or an entire quarter's memory work—or random verses.

Instructions:

Fold white paper accordion fashion according to the width of the pattern you are using. Trace the pattern onto tagboard. Cut out and use for making your folded paper. Cut out the pattern and unfold. You may then decide to trim every third or fourth icicle to a shorter length for variety and a more natural appearance.

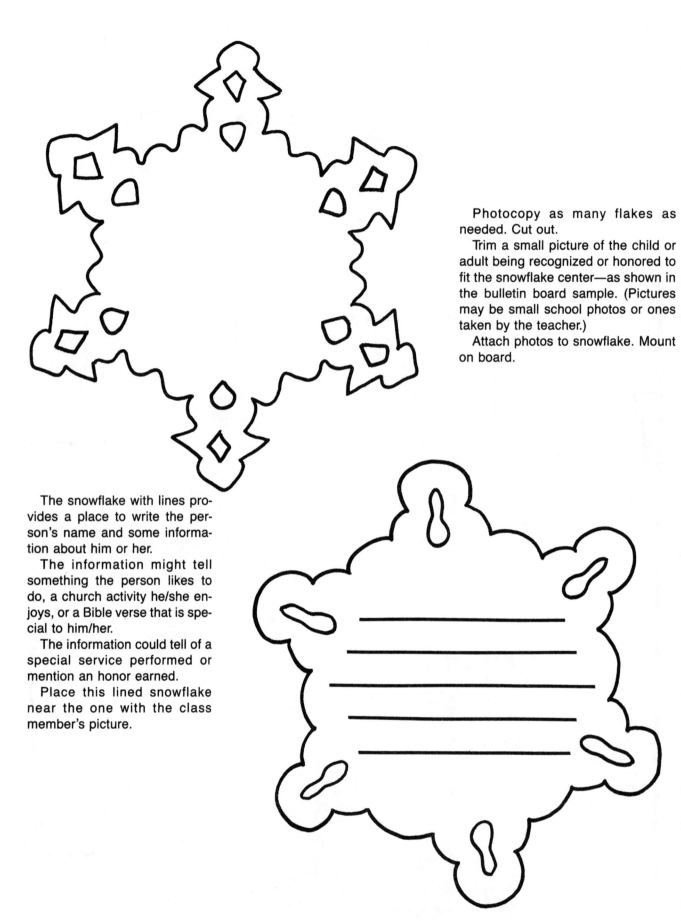

Photocopy as many flakes as needed. Cut out.

Trim a small picture of the child or adult being recognized or honored to fit the snowflake center—as shown in the bulletin board sample. (Pictures may be small school photos or ones taken by the teacher.)

Attach photos to snowflake. Mount on board.

The snowflake with lines provides a place to write the person's name and some information about him or her.

The information might tell something the person likes to do, a church activity he/she enjoys, or a Bible verse that is special to him/her.

The information could tell of a special service performed or mention an honor earned.

Place this lined snowflake near the one with the class member's picture.

JESUS—

the light of the world

"Later, Jesus talked to the people again. He said, 'I am the light of the world. The person who follows me will never live in darkness. He will have the light that gives life.'"

—John 8:12

Suggestions

Background—blue

Candle—white, yellow for flame, pattern on page fifty-eight

Ribbon—three inch wide red ribbon or crepe paper fastened to board as shown

Branches—real evergreen or bush branches slant pinned to board, *or,* green paper branches, pattern on page sixty

Letters—yellow or red, patterns for enlarging on page sixty-one.

Verse booklets—patterns and instructions on pages fifty-six, fifty-seven

Instructions:

Cut out candle booklet cover and worksheet.

Students write verse on worksheet.

Fold cover tab back. Fold worksheet tab forward. (The verse will be *inside,* facing the cover.) Glue. Tie yellow ribbon through both candle flames to close booklet.

Students may color booklet cover.

Alternate use:

May use as a Christmas card. Cover top line and word, ''verse,'' and the word ''name'' at the bottom before photocopying.

Fold back on dotted line. Glue to tab of worksheet candle.

Verse

Example

NAME

Fold forward on dotted line. Glue to tab of illustrated candle.

PATTERNS

Pages fifty-eight through sixty-one are the patterns for use on many of the bulletin boards in this book.

These four pages are designed to be made into overhead transparencies.

When the transparency is placed on an overhead projector, the patterns can be enlarged to the exact board size desired.

LEARNING TO OBEY GOD

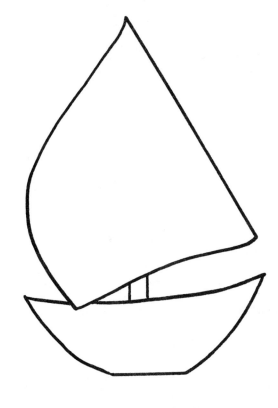

A Piggy Bank
for
Jesus

Jesus Lives!

Jesus, Rose of Sharon

Book Nook

JESUS—
the light of the world

A Child's Garden of Verses

"Berry" Good Birthdays!   Behavior

Memorization   Books   Deeds   Art

Notes

Jesus in My Heart

News

Ideas

Winter WonderKIDS

A Money Tree for Jesus

PRAYER

HAS

A GREAT REVIEW

WINGS!

THANKSgiving   Summertime

For Dad

World

We Love Mom   Missions

Blank Calendar Form

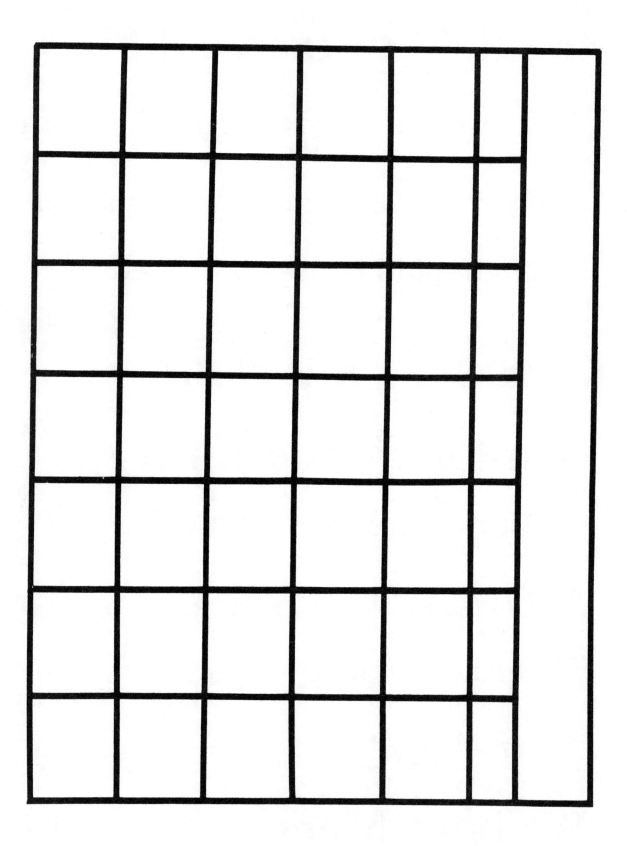

Blank Card Form

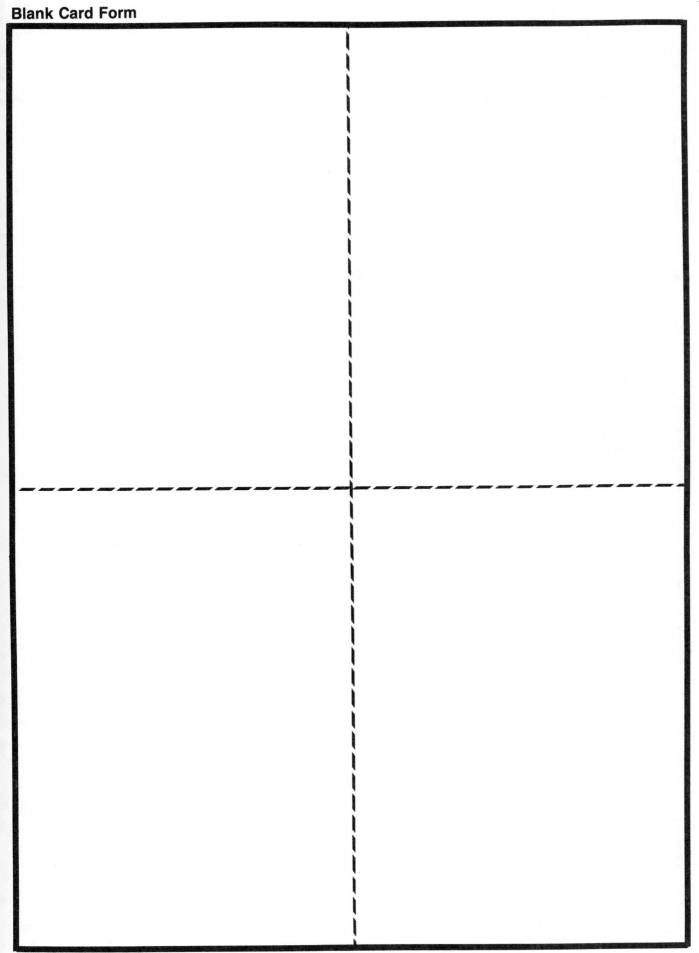

Blank Puzzle Form

Uses—Students may write memory verses on puzzle, cut apart, and put verse back together.
  —Students may draw a review picture of the lesson, cut apart, and put together.

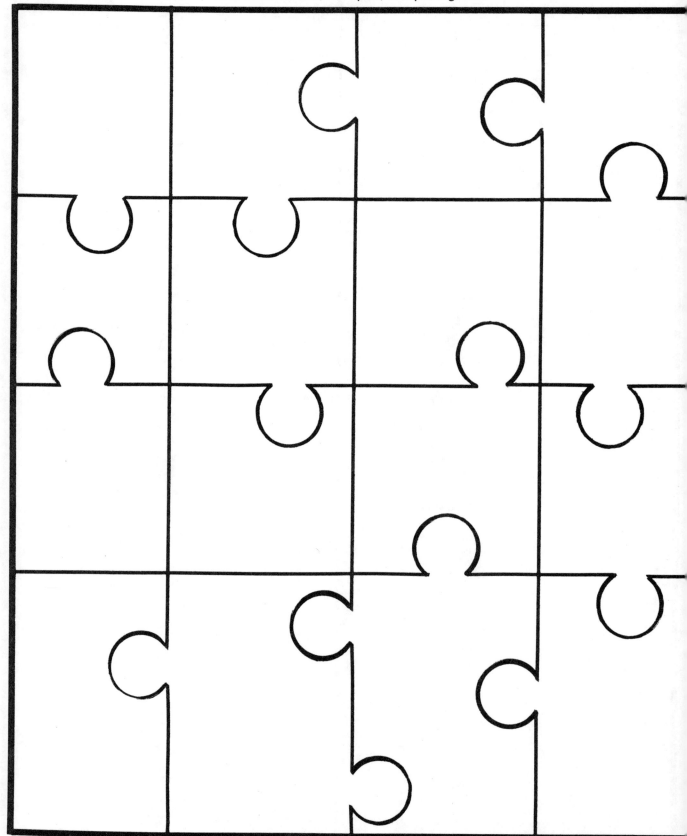